HOW TO PASS ELITE FORCES SELECTION

ELITE FORCES SURVIVAL GUIDE SERIES

Elite Survival
Survive in the Desert with the French Foreign Legion
Survive in the Arctic with the Royal Marine Commandos
Survive in the Mountains with the U.S. Rangers and Army
   Mountain Division
Survive in the Jungle with the Special Forces "Green Berets"
Survive in the Wilderness with the Canadian and Australian
   Special Forces
Survive at Sea with the U.S. Navy SEALs
Training to Fight with the Parachute Regiment
The World's Best Soldiers

Elite Operations and Training
Escape and Evasion
Surviving Captivity with the U.S. Air Force
Hostage Rescue with the SAS
How to Pass Elite Forces Selection
Learning Mental Endurance with the U.S. Marines

Special Forces Survival Guidebooks
Survival Equipment
Navigation and Signaling
Surviving Natural Disasters
Using Ropes and Knots
Survival First Aid
Trapping, Fishing, and Plant Food
Urban Survival Techniques

HOW TO PASS ELITE FORCES SELECTION

CHRIS McNAB

Introduction by Colonel John T. Carney. Jr., USAF–Ret.
President, Special Operations Warrior Foundation

MASON CREST PUBLISHERS

This edition first published in 2003
by Mason Crest Publishers Inc.
370 Reed Road, Broomall, PA, 19008

Library of Congress Cataloging-in-Publication Data available

ISBN 1-59084-012-7

Editorial and design by
Amber Books Ltd.
Bradley's Close
74–77 White Lion Street
London N1 9PF

Project Editor Chris Stone
Designer Simon Thompson
Picture Research Lisa Wren

Printed and bound in Malaysia

10 9 8 7 6 5 4 3 2 1

ACKNOWLEDGMENT
For authenticating this book, the Publishers would like to thank the Public Affairs Offices of the U.S. Special Operations Command, MacDill AFB, FL.; Army Special Operations Command, Fort Bragg, N.C.; Navy Special Warfare Command, Coronado, CA.; and the Air Force Special Operations Command, Hurlbert Field, FL.

IMPORTANT NOTICE
The survival techniques and information described in this publication are for use in dire circumstances where the safety of the individual is at risk. Accordingly, the publisher cannot accept any responsibility for any prosecution or proceedings brought or instituted against any person or body as a result of the uses or misuses of the techniques and information within.

DEDICATION
This book is dedicated to those who perished in the terrorist attacks of September 11, 2001, and to the Special Forces soldiers who continually serve to defend freedom.

Picture Credits
Corbis: 6, 8, 14, 16, 22, 44, 47, 48, 49, 50, 55; **Military Picture Library**: 26, 28, 34, 36, 39
TRH: 12, 18, 29, 31, 52, 54; **US Dept. of Defense**: 10, 20, 24.
Illustrations courtesy of Amber Books and the following supplied by Patrick Mulrey: 32.
Front cover: **TRH** (inset), **Military Picture Library** (main)

CONTENTS

Introduction   6

The Importance of Being Fit   8

Preparing the Mind   18

How Elite Units are Chosen   26

SAS Selection   34

Special Forces Selection   42

U.S. Navy SEALs Selection   50

Glossary   58

Recruitment Information   60

Further Reading/About the Author   63

Index   64

INTRODUCTION

Elite forces are the tip of Freedom's spear. These small, special units are universally the first to engage, whether on reconnaissance missions into denied territory for larger, conventional forces or in direct action, surgical operations, preemptive strikes, retaliatory action, and hostage rescues. They lead the way in today's war on terrorism, the war on drugs, the war on transnational unrest, and in humanitarian operations as well as nation building. When large scale warfare erupts, they offer theater commanders a wide variety of unique, unconventional options.

Most such units are regionally oriented, acclimated to the culture and conversant in the languages of the areas where they operate. Since they deploy to those areas regularly, often for combined training exercises with indigenous forces, these elite units also serve as peacetime "global scouts" and "diplomacy multipliers," a beacon of hope for the democratic aspirations of oppressed peoples all over the globe.

Elite forces are truly "quiet professionals": their actions speak louder than words. They are self-motivated, self-confident, versatile, seasoned, mature individuals who rely on teamwork more than daring-do. Unfortunately, theirs is dangerous work. Since "Desert One"—the 1980 attempt to rescue hostages from the U.S. embassy in Tehran, for instance—American special operations forces have suffered casualties in real world operations at close to fifteen times the rate of U.S. conventional forces. By the very nature of the challenges which face special operations forces, training for these elite units has proven even more hazardous.

Thus it's with special pride that I join you in saluting the brave men and women who volunteer to serve in and support these magnificent units and who face such difficult challenges ahead.

Colonel John T. Carney, Jr., USAF–Ret.
President, Special Operations Warrior Foundation

A Marine recruit scales a climbing wall at the Recruit Depot, Parris Island, South Carolina.

THE IMPORTANCE OF BEING FIT

To enter an elite unit, you need to be super fit. Special Forces soldiers have to be able to keep going when regular people fail. That is why they must train their minds and bodies for maximum endurance and strength.

It is strange that people may spend lots of time and effort cleaning their cars, but they often neglect the most valuable possession they will ever have—their bodies. Elite soldiers are different. They spend a large part of their time training their bodies for top performance. If Special Forces soldiers do not have strong minds in healthy bodies, then chances are they will fail in their missions. In this chapter, we will look at what you should do to get fit for elite forces selection, and how to keep fit in the long term.

The healthier you are, the more you are likely to enjoy life to the fullest. Keeping good health also helps avoid illness and injuries. Medical science has shown that if you keep fit and try to eat a healthy diet, you stand a better chance of living longer. In extreme situations, such as those faced by elite soldiers, your level of fitness and overall health can make the difference between living and dying.

You may be aware of the effect of stress in your life. Stress is something that affects most people at some time. The elite soldier or

Physical training at Marine boot camp. Leg exercises are particularly vital, since the soldier may need to swim great distances.

the high school student around exam time can experience different types of stress, but the effect will be same. If you suffer from a poor appetite, interrupted sleep, feelings of unease or of not being in control of your life, or just a general lack of confidence, getting fit will certainly help you. Everyone can improve their lifestyle and get greater enjoyment just by following a simple fitness program.

Fitness can be broken down into three categories: **suppleness**, **stamina**, and strength. Younger people often place emphasis on

Elite training can be too much even for the strongest of men. This U.S. soldier is helped by medics after becoming exhausted during a 10-mile (16-km) run. Getting fit takes time and cannot be rushed.

strength and stamina, while older people may want to spend more time on improving suppleness. Nevertheless, suppleness is important for all of us, and it is especially important in self-defense where high kicks might be needed. Running speed and fighting power also depend on a high degree of suppleness. If you begin every exercise program with a gentle warm-up and a series of stretching exercises, blood starts to flow to the muscles and you can help avoid the muscle tears and strained **ligaments** caused by sudden physical movements. Also, after a tough exercise session you must cool down with a series of gentle exercises, so your body can return to normal.

Pace yourself

Too much exercise too soon can lead to an injury. Begin slowly and gradually build up the speed and the number of times you repeat any exercise. If you have not exercised for some time, start by taking fast walks. Walk home from school, rather than catch the bus. Use the stairs instead of taking the elevator. Walk to the corner store instead of going in the car. Do a little exercise every day and you will soon experience the benefit. Do not be discouraged by the initial discomfort; it is always hard work when you begin. You will soon get into a routine and the aches will disappear as your fitness increases.

If you start to experience chest-pains, pains shooting up the arms, problems with breathing, sweating, or headaches, see your doctor.

When trying to get fit, it is important to select the right gym, though your school may have its own facilities. It often pays to visit different gyms before making your selection. Of course, you can

"Mudwalking" requires soldiers to struggle through chest-high mud for hundreds of feet (tens of meters), and is particularly hard on the legs. This exercise is part of U.S. Navy SEAL's basic training period.

always train at home, but lack of space may be a problem. In good weather, you can use the backyard. Self-motivation may be another problem—at home there are no gym instructors to spur you on.

Before doing any hard exercise, you must warm up first to prevent your muscles from getting damaged. Any mild exercise, such as jogging, is an ideal warm-up, but it is important to pay attention to all the muscles in your body. Walking, swimming, and cycling are ideal ways to warm up, as long as you take it gently. The general idea is to raise the pulse and get the blood circulating. The length of time spent warming up will depend on the temperature of the place in which you are exercising. On a warm day, the minimum warm-up period is about six minutes, but on a cold day you will need to exercise for at least 12 minutes.

Here is a good way of warming up using the running track in a regular gym:

- For the first three laps, stay on your toes and lift your knees high.
- On the fourth lap, start to exercise the arms, punching the arms high in the air, first with the left arm and then with the right.
- On lap five, face inward and run sideways, leading with the left leg. Halfway through the lap, face outward so that your right leg leads.
- On lap six, hop for 33 feet (10 m) on one leg, then change to the other leg and repeat.
- On lap seven, run backward for half a lap and then forward again, punching your arms above your head. Watch where you're going.

Repeated kicking of a heavy punch bag is a way of fostering controlled physical aggression in every elite recruit.

- After seven laps, stand with your legs a shoulder's width apart, with your hands on hips and elbows slightly forward. Breathe deeply and slowly, in through the nose and out through the mouth. This warm-up period helps soldiers prevent injury and prepares the body for more demanding exercise. You should never skip the warm-up—elite soldiers do it before every exercise routine.

Now that the body is warmed up, it is time to start stretching your muscles, **tendons**, and ligaments to improve overall mobility and to help flexibility. When stretching, always start at the top and work down the body. You must learn stretching skills from a fitness instructor because it is very important that it is done properly or you can hurt yourself. Ask your coach, trainer, or physical therapy trainer for information about how to stretch. The most important thing to remember is that you do not stretch too hard—if it hurts a lot, then stop.

Exercise must be fun, otherwise you will not want to continue doing it regularly. Try to exercise with a group of friends. Exercising to exciting music makes it all the more enjoyable. A lot of people say that they dislike exercise, either because of bad experiences at

U.S. Navy SEAL BUDS perform calisthenics (in this case, push-ups) next to the pool at the North Island Naval Air Station in California.

school or for other reasons. It is hard work but, of course, almost anything worthwhile has a price. The more you do, the easier it becomes and the more you will enjoy it. It is a good habit that can even become an addiction.

When training for elite forces selection, the main things to focus on are speed, strength, and endurance. There is a wide range of exercises you can do to build these three qualities:

Calisthenics

These are the rigid, military-type, "parade ground" exercises, designed to promote straight backs, raised chests, and a shoulders-back physique. Some people think that it is cool to slouch, but not elite soldiers. They take pride in themselves and want to look and feel like a soldier. As the old saying goes, "If you look good, you feel good."

Anaerobic exercise

Anaerobic exercises tend to be fast, furious, and short, and you generally do not get out of breath. Anaerobic exercises include martial arts and sprinting over short distances (no more than 100 meters). Anaerobic exercises are good for building up muscle strength, but not good for endurance—that needs **aerobic** exercises.

Aerobic exercise

Most exercise is aerobic, because it makes your heart beat faster and your lungs breathe more deeply. Aerobic exercise also includes endurance workouts such as rowing, cycling, and swimming, plus the longer track events such as the 800 and 1,500 meters. Aerobic

Lifting weights—as demonstrated by this U.S. soldier taking a break from Operation "Desert Storm" in 1991—builds up muscle strength and helps the soldier lift the huge weights carried into battle.

exercise helps build up heart and lung strength, which is vital if you are to succeed the elite forces selection.

Circuit training

Circuit training involves doing lots of different exercises that strengthen all parts of your body. In one part of the gym you might jog on the spot, then run to another spot where you do stomach exercises. Circuits often use weights and exercise machines.

Weight training

This increases performance by increasing overall strength. It is important because elite forces soldiers have to carry very heavy weights into battle—sometimes their packs and rifles can add up to 80 pounds (36 kg) in weight. Most gyms and some schools have weight rooms, but make sure that an experienced instructor shows you what to do first.

This is a good piece of overall advice for getting fit: talk to a qualified, official fitness instructor and ask him or her what exercises you need to do to get really strong, flexible, and fit. Once you start to exercise, you will feel healthier, happier, and stronger. If you attempt Special Forces selection in the future, you are going to need to be incredibly fit, so start training now.

STRETCHING YOUR HEAD AND NECK

- Stand with hands on hips and legs one shoulder's width apart. Rotate your head in a large circle and brush your upper chest with your chin, but do not tip your head too far back . Do six repetitions clockwise and six counterclockwise.
- Turn the head left and right, trying to see as far behind you as possible without moving your shoulders. Work up to 12 repetitions. Do this slowly at first. As your neck becomes more flexible, you will be able to do this at a faster rate.
- Bend your head forward until your chin touches the chest. Flex the head back until you are looking at the sky. Repeat the exercise, starting to move your head to the right (as far as is comfortable). Do six "nods" to the left and six to the right.

PREPARING THE MIND

Because elite forces selection is so challenging, you have to have a tough mind as well as a strong body. Only by being confident, believing in yourself, and showing courage, do you stand a good chance of making it through the elites' toughest training exercises.

Positive thinking is the key to success in dealing with the dangerous or frightening situations that elite soldiers face. To pass Special Forces training, recruits have to be positive about life; they have to believe in themselves. In order to do this, they have to work to eliminate weaknesses and make themselves better. Life in a competitive world is hard. Recruits are aware of their limitations and resolve to do something about them.

To start your fitness program, you need motivation. Simply being unfit may supply the necessary motivation. You can become annoyed about running out of breath easily or constantly feeling tired. Compare yourself with other people of the same age and sex. Are they healthier and happier than you? Select a person who you admire greatly and ask yourself what it is that you admire. You will have many of the same qualities, although, perhaps, they are not so obvious. If this was not true, you would not admire these qualities; other people are mirrors in which you can see yourself. However, do not just copy other people. Work out what it is that

Push-ups test both stamina and strength—elite soldiers must be able to do at least 42 full push-ups in two minutes.

You do not need to join a gym to get fit. These U.S. Marines from Third Platoon, India Company, race around the flight deck of the U.S.S. Guam as part of their continuing training.

you like about this individual and concentrate on developing these qualities in yourself. Also, look at what is weak about this person and ask yourself if you have these weaknesses too.

Once you have begun your training program, you can start to experiment with different exercise routines to suit you. We are all different and we all have individual needs. Think hard about your goals and then go for them. Set yourself sensible challenges and celebrate when you achieve them. It is all too easy to concentrate only on those activities you enjoy or are good at. Ask your best friend or a training companion to tell you how you are improving. Ask their advice on how they would modify your training program. Share your life experiences and problems with them.

Criticism can be painful but, providing that it is constructive and helpful criticism, it can help you to see yourself as other people see you. There will be times when you will be tested by life. Things will go wrong and you must be prepared for this to happen. Try to imagine the very worst that could happen to you, then force yourself to imagine coping with this situation. When you are doing the Special Forces endurance walks, imagine getting

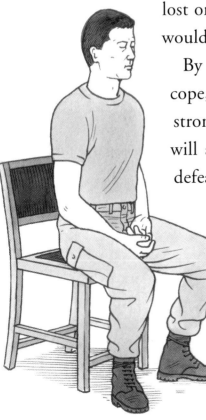

lost on the hills or breaking your leg. How would you then cope with bad weather?

By simply imagining how you would cope, you are training your mind to be strong. The soldier with a strong character will always be able to bounce back from defeat. After a setback, your motivation should become even stronger.

The final key to motivation is personal enjoyment. It may not always seem possible to

Through the powers of self-hypnosis and positive thinking, the recruit can "will" himself to perform better.

"I can't hear you!" All Marines must shout out their responses during training. It shows that they are committed to what they are doing and have respect for their officers.

look forward to a hard training session, but once the session is over you should be left with a warm glow of satisfaction and accomplishment.

Fitness training will make you more confident. It should leave you feeling healthy and with a more pleasing self-image. Energy will appear to radiate from you. Knowing that you can project a confident image can be useful in many situations. It may enable you to control an encounter with a bullying person or to deal with a tough interview. You may well be experiencing anxiety and fear. You cannot help how you feel, but you can help what you do about these feelings. Fear must be controlled and this is an important part of projecting a confident self-image.

One of the most unexpected qualities of an elite soldier is a sense of humor. A sense of humor is vital to success. We all suffer setbacks, and it is often just when you think that you are winning that disaster strikes. Humor helps us to feel better about our troubles. A British Special Air Service (**SAS**) patrol up to their necks in swamp water and leeches will look at each other and laugh. Why not? No amount of cursing or complaining will alter their situation. You just have to laugh it off and push on. If you can develop the ability to laugh at yourself, you will never get so angry that you lose control. Remember, it is as easy to be happy in this world as it is to be miserable. If you can think positively, keep on moving forward, and laugh when disaster strikes, you will eventually attain your goals.

In your mind you must have a clear picture of what you want to achieve, especially if you are going for elite forces training. Aim high, but be realistic. Chart a course that will get you what you want and take it one step at a time. Expect setbacks and always have plans for when things go wrong. Only you can help achieve your dreams. Do not make excuses for not doing things. Never leave jobs until tomorrow.

To be as good as an SAS soldier, you must be dedicated and be prepared to put in the time and effort. Nothing that is really worthwhile in life comes easily. If you want it badly enough, you can get it.

Fear is another obstacle we must all face and overcome, particularly in the Special Forces. First, do not be ashamed of fear. It is a natural response that comes into play when you see a threat, whether it is real or imagined. It is just unfortunate that, while the sudden jolt of fear was a real lifesaver for our prehistoric ancestors, it may have outlived its usefulness. Here are two tips

Armed Marines undergo training in hostage rescue at Camp Lejeune, North Carolina, May 1997. Only soldiers who have stable emotions can deal professionally with situations as demanding as this.

HANDLING PANIC

Panic is one of the most destructive emotions. It should never be tolerated. A Japanese psychiatrist found the following three-step exercise can be very successful in helping his patients cope with panic. It can be used in every situation.

1 Stand or sit upright.

2 Take a deep breath through the mouth, filling your lungs.

3 Exhale very slowly through the nose. Imagine that you are holding a feather in front of your nose and exhale so gently that the "feather" remains perfectly still.

for overcoming personal fear:

• Try to put your problems into perspective. Very few incidents or decisions have a lasting effect on our lives. Become philosophical about life, and think of it as a constant cycle of joy and sorrow, success and defeat, frustration and achievement. Do not worry needlessly about life's problems.

• Imagine yourself confronting a situation that makes you feel anxious. Play it through in your mind and imagine getting the better of the situation. We all experience fear; some of us are just better at coping with it or disguising it.

Confidence is the greatest enemy of fear. Use elite forces training to help attain your goals. Achievement, fulfillment, and inner happiness are the ingredients that create confidence.

HOW ELITE UNITS ARE CHOSEN

Selection procedures for elite units are tough to make sure that only those recruits with great mental and physical stamina succeed. These are men and women who can keep on going when others want to give up, and who have the intelligence to operate sophisticated weapons and tools.

Units such as the British SAS, American **Special Forces** and **SEALs**, and Russian **Spetsnaz** forces have set standards of excellence for Special Forces. As a result, selection and training methods—though each unit has its own program—have many similarities the world over.

The people who choose elite soldiers are looking for two main sets of qualities. The first is required of all battlefield elites: aggression, physical fitness, and team spirit. The second set of qualities is related to character. Most modern elite units fight in small, independent groups either at the forefront of the battle or behind enemy lines. Such soldiers must have a high degree of self-discipline, motivation, intelligence, and initiative. In combat they must be dependable, self-reliant, and masters of modern equipment, weapons, field tactics, and many other specialized skills needed for their work.

The two biggest hurdles facing an applicant for an elite unit are first, finding the courage to "give it a try" and, second, hanging in

A Russian Spetsnaz soldier practices "fire-running," which is entering a burning building during hostage-rescue training (Kiev, 1996).

Kit inspection is a testing time. Clothing must be cleaned and ironed, boots polished, and equipment arranged neatly within the backpack so the soldier can display it at a moment's notice.

there when the going gets tough. The going gets tough quickly for new arrivals to Britain's Parachute Regiment. They leave the comforts of home, the right to do what they want when they want, and a familiar pattern of life. In return, recruit training offers an iron regime that starts at **0700 hours** and ends at 2000 hours—13 hours of hard soldiering and fitness training.

In reality, the day does not finish at 2000 hours. The recruits' notebooks are full of memos taken during lessons on infantry weapons and **kit**. This all needs to be memorized. There are lockers to be tidied, boots to be highly polished, and uniforms to be washed and ironed. Finally, they prepare their kit for the next morning. Perhaps for the first time in their lives, they are faced with paying for what they lose. Much worse is the threat of having to explain the loss at the next kit inspection, or going on a field exercise without an essential item of kit such as a water bottle. If the drill instructor discovers items are missing, the recruit can expect public ridicule together with an impossible number of push-ups.

The recruits' worst enemy at this stage of their training is the knowledge that they can be thrown off the course at any time. Up

The "Log Race" takes place on the Friday of Week 12 of Para training. Many recruits, already exhausted after completing the Steeplechase that morning, fail the course.

until Week Eight all recruits can pay money to leave. Many use that right. The final straw might come on a wet night in the field when, already exhausted, they are woken up at 0200 hours to take their turn on guard duty, or when a 10-mile (16-km) speed march continues past the usual finishing point and onto the assault course.

At the end of Week Four, the survivors go onto the endurance phase called **"P" Company**. Now only the strongest remain. Thoughts of leaving are gone—ahead lies the famous red beret if they can survive. "P" Company not only continues to develop the recruits' infantry skills, but also concentrates on the recruits' character and motivation. It involves hard speed marches across mountains, mixed with adventure training. After a brief interlude on the ranges to test the recruits' marksmanship and weapons handling, Week 12 or "Test Week" arrives all too quickly.

On the Friday morning the recruits face the **"Steeplechase"**—a test of individual effort and physical fitness. To pass, a recruit must twice run over a four-fifths of a mile (1.3-km) obstacle course in an average time of 17.5 minutes. The next event is a test of team effort and real endurance—the **"log race."** A team of eight recruits must carry a log the size of a telegraph pole weighing approximately 655 pounds (295 kg) over a one-and-three-quarters–mile (2.8-km) course of sand hills in 12 to 14 minutes. The recruits experience a "world of pain" in this test designed to simulate pulling an antitank gun into action. Letting go of the rope results in two dreadful penalties: first, the person automatically fails "P" Company and second, that individual lets down the rest of the team, because they have to struggle to the finish line with one less person to help.

On Monday, the selection process starts again as the recruits are faced with completing the classic 10-mile (16-km) battle march. Encumbered with a backpack and rifle—weighing nearly 48 pounds (22 kg)—the squad must run most of the way to complete this test in the time of 105 minutes. Already exhausted, the recruits are immediately marched onto the "**Trainasium.**" The Trainasium is a structure of scaffolding poles and narrow catwalks, 35 to 50 feet (9.5–15 m) high and cunningly constructed to test the recruits' nerve and reaction to orders. After leaping gaps, crawling across wires, and

Following the Log Race, recruits take part in "milling." It might look like boxing, but there is no ducking or weaving allowed—it is full-on combat, testing aggression and endurance in equal measure.

standing on the 50-foot (15-m) "shuffle-bars," the recruits face a jump across a gap of eight and a quarter feet (2.5 m). On each obstacle, the recruits have just three opportunities to overcome their fear, a mental process that they will need to repeat every time they arrive at the open door of an aircraft.

This phase of "P" Company ends with the assault course, after which the recruits are treated to further endurance marches and another stretcher race. Now the recruits have their red berets and are sent to the Royal Air Force's No. 1 Parachute School to earn their parachute wings. The novice paratroopers learn to land correctly and cope with several types of potentially fatal midair emergencies. Then the students make practice jumps from the indoor descent trainer and

Elite soldiers must be intelligent. Behind enemy lines they will need to work out complex compass coordinates and calculate the trajectory of missiles, so advanced proficiency in math is essential.

TIPS FOR COMPLETING ENDURANCE MARCHES

- Keep out of rivers and streams; they can be difficult to cross and the water may be very fast and cold.
- Climb very steep hills on a diagonal route or by zig-zagging—it takes less energy than walking straight up.
- Watch where you place your foot and make sure that every foothold is secure before you put your weight on it.
- Never walk with your hands in your pockets.
- Try to cover as much ground as possible with each stride.

the 72-foot (22-m) tower, before readying themselves for a parachute jump from a hot air balloon flying 2,624 feet (800 m) above the ground. This prepares the recruits for the main event. At the end of 20 days of training they will have completed eight parachute jumps from an aircraft, including jumps at night. More advanced infantry training with their battalions lies ahead. After two to three years experience in a rifle company, there is the possibility of further specialized training with the numerous support platoons and sections.

The Paras training gives you an idea of what is needed to pass elite forces selection. You need to be very physically fit, mentally strong, and determined to succeed. However, there are even tougher training courses around the world. In the rest of this book, we will look at what it takes to pass the selection courses for three of the most elite units in the world—the Special Air Service (SAS), the Special Forces, and the U.S. Navy SEALs.

SAS SELECTION

22 SAS is the world's most famous elite unit, made up of approximately 80 men. The SAS draws its recruits from the other regiments and corps of the British Army—selection and training lasts almost two years and is designed to weed out all but the strongest fighters.

The SAS soldier is someone who is self-motivated and able to think for himself. For many applicants, passing into the Regiment will mean breaking the habits of a lifetime, since soldiers in most other regiments are conditioned to rely heavily on their officers for orders and direction. The SAS soldier stands on his own two feet.

While waiting for a place on a winter or summer selection course, most serious candidates start to develop their physical fitness and stamina on long runs. Solo walks across the high mountains of Wales not only train the soldiers in navigation, but also introduce them to hardship and the process of self-reliance. These qualities are valued by the SAS selection staff.

On their arrival at the Regiment's home base in Hereford, England, the candidates face a short build-up period of road runs and cross-country marches—two weeks for officers and three weeks for others. Then they face the exhausting marches of "final selection," and arrive at what is called Test Week physically and mentally exhausted. Ahead of them lie several 19- to 25-mile (30–40 km)

An SAS soldier aims his M16 rifle through bushes during an escape and evasion exercise as part of Continuation Training in Borneo, 1999.

During final selection for the SAS in the Brecon Becons, Wales. With mountains reaching up to 2,660 feet (811 m), recruits are tested in wet-weather survival and exposure to cold-water rivers.

forced marches culminating in the "Fan Dance" or "Long Drag"—a 37$^{1}/_{2}$-mile (60-km) forced march over some of the highest peaks in Wales, to be completed in around 20 hours carrying a 55-pound (25-kg) bergen (backpack). The candidates are expected to navigate their way through a series of rendezvous (**RV**) points. At every RV, each person is checked for signs of illness, but neither the hot, drying winds of summer, nor the cruel blizzards of winter stop the course. Ahead lies an unknown number of RVs and mountain ridges to be crossed. Those with the sheer willpower to keep concentrating, while putting one foot in front of the other to keep up the pace, will pass.

The 10 percent or less who complete the endurance walks are now faced with learning the essential skills for behind-the-lines operations on a 14-week course known as "**Continuation Training.**" The physical pressure has eased, but there are still mental hurdles to be crossed and the candidates can still fail the selection process. Small patrol tactics have to be learned and practiced until they become second nature. The students learn the techniques that will let the patrol survive surprise contact with the enemy. They are taught how to remain unseen and what to carry in their backpacks so that they can survive for weeks in enemy territory.

The signals course introduces the students to the basic principles of undercover communications, Morse code, and the great variety of radio transmitters employed by the SAS. For many, the biggest hurdle will be learning to recognize the sound of high-speed Morse as letters and words, rather than a series of dots and dashes. To pass the course, the men must be able to transmit and receive Morse code at a speed of eight words per minute, which is the standard rate for British Army Regimental Signalers.

A high level of medical skill is also essential for elite soldiers. This is because they often operate deep behind enemy lines where there are no army hospitals and rescue is difficult. From learning basic first aid, the students progress to more advanced lifesaving techniques usually performed by qualified doctors: from mending broken limbs to treating a range of infectious diseases.

After a short period of demolitions training, the students find themselves learning the art of combat survival. Lighting fires, catching animals, building survival shelters, and staying out of the hands of the enemy prepare the students for being cut off behind enemy lines. A week's survival course in the wilder areas of the ·United Kingdom not only provides the opportunity to test these skills, but also prepares them for a short escape and evasion/resistance to interrogation (RTI) exercise. In common with pilots and other soldiers who work behind enemy lines, the SAS

A .—	M — —	Y —.— —
B —...	N —.	Z — —..—
C —.—.	O — — —	1 .— — — —
D —..	P .— —.	2 ..— —
E .	Q — —.—	3 ...— —
F ..—.	R .—.	4 ....—
G — —.	S ...	5 .....
H	T —	6 —....
I ..	U ..—	7 — —...
J .— — —	V ...—	8 — — —..
K —.—	W .— —	9 — — — —.
L .—..	X —..—	0 — — — — —

Morse code is the most reliable method of covert communication. There are even special signals for foreign letters, so soldiers can understand the exact spelling of unusual names and places.

During hostage-rescue missions, often the only entry to a building is by abseiling (descending by the use of a rope) down the walls from the roof. Prospective SAS soldiers practice abseiling skills on the cliffs of Wales during final selection.

troopers must be given every opportunity to avoid capture. If a soldier is taken, he must be able to resist the threats and physical and mental brutality of the interrogators. The surrendering of any military information, however insignificant, may well lead to the deaths of other patrol members.

A jungle-training phase followed by a parachuting course complete SAS Continuation Training. Even at this late stage, applicants can still fail the selection procedure. Entire patrols that became lost during jungle training have been failed. The parachute course makes further demands on the student's confidence and his ability to control fear. Although selection and Continuation Training are now officially over, the trooper goes on to serve a one-year period with one of the Regiment's operational or "Sabre" Squadrons, in which the soldier has to prove he is good enough for the SAS. For the 12 months, he will

An SAS operative in the Falkland Islands armed with a Colt Commando XM117 assault rifle.

concentrate in depth on one of the essential patrol skills: medicine, demolitions, languages, or communications. Equally important are his troop skills. Each Sabre Squadron is divided into four 16-man units, with each one having a specialty: parachuting, small boat/combat swimmer operations, mountain and winter warfare, and long-range vehicle operations.

The three-year tour of duty cycle is almost at an end before the SAS soldier has had a chance to learn all the new skills and tasks expected of him. Officers must return to their original British Army units at the end of their tour. The enlisted men can opt for a further three years of duty, with the promise of more advanced training.

ELITE ENDURANCE

During the Gulf War in 1991, an SAS soldier called Chris Ryan used his SAS training to conquer adverse conditions and survive. While behind enemy lines in Iraq, his patrol was ambushed by Iraqi troops. Ryan was separated from the rest of the men. He had little food or water with him, and what he did have was soon used up. By the third day, he was mentally and physically shattered, but he refused to give up and carried on. Soon his feet were cut and bleeding. By the sixth day, he was severely dehydrated. He came across a stream and drank from it, but it was poisoned and he became ill. After seven nights and eight days, he reached the Syrian border and safety. He had walked a total of 186 miles (300 km).

SPECIAL FORCES SELECTION

The U.S. Special Forces rose to fame in the Vietnam War. During that conflict they terrorized the enemy deep in the heart of the jungle. Since then, they have proved themselves to be expert soldiers in many types of war.

Being accepted for selection for the American Special Forces is almost as tough as passing their infamous course—they number approximately 7,200 in all, including reserves. Most of the enlisted candidates who are accepted for Special Forces selection are sergeants with a minimum of three years service. Officers must wait until their fourth year of service before applying for the Special Forces. All candidates must be able to swim 164 feet (50 m) in boots and clothing, pass a general medical, and obtain the necessary security clearance. In addition, they must be high school graduates and have passed their advanced physical readiness test, advanced military training, and junior NCOs school (E4–E7). Applicants must be qualified in using parachutes and most have successfully completed Ranger School at Fort Benning, if not actually having served with the 75th Ranger Regiment. Not surprisingly, most successful applicants are drawn from the infantry and other combat arms of the Army.

On arrival at Camp MacKall, North Carolina, applicants face a tough 25-day preselection course called Special Forces

This Special Forces captain from 1965 wears the first issue of official kit sent to troops in Vietnam, indicated by the slanted shirt pockets.

The Special Forces soldiers' mock parachute jump often takes place only inches (a few centimeters) off the ground. It drills soldiers in the correct technique and builds their confidence.

Assessment and Selection (SFAS). Twenty-five days of continuous mental and physical stress persuade the poorly motivated to leave at the beginning of the selection process. Only about half of an average class of 300 candidates pass SFAS and win a place on the Special Forces Qualification Course ("Q" Course).

The course is divided into a further three phases: Small Unit Tactics, Military Occupational Skill (MOS) Specific Training, and a Culmination Exercise that includes a field exercise called "Robin Sage," where the candidates will be asked to demonstrate all the skills they have learned on the course. The Small Unit Tactics phase lasts 46 days. It concentrates on the basic crafts for a career behind enemy lines. The candidates are taught navigation, field craft, unarmed combat, small unit tactics, and live-fire exercises. During this phase, the selectors watch the candidates carefully. They not only note the applicant's ability to absorb information, but they also watch the student's discipline and self-reliance. Special Forces selection is almost unique in the U.S. Army in that the students are not subjected to any external pressure or pep talks. Like the SAS, self-motivation is vital to training.

At the beginning of the next phase, the students are divided up into groups, each training in different skills: weapons, communications, engineering, or combat medicine. This will be the soldier's essential role within his 12-man "A-Team" unit. Officers have their own training detachment, which teaches more advanced combat tactics. Combat medicine is the longest course. It lasts for 21 weeks, and is held at the John F. Kennedy Special Warfare Center and School (SWCS). There, the students are asked to take a "mini-medical degree," which covers everything from **anatomy** and **physiology** to veterinary medicine and war surgery. Each day begins at 0430 hours and ends long after dark, when the students are given time for private study. The course is so difficult that one commanding officer at the school has said that most medical students would fail the Special Forces medical course.

The other courses last for 65 days. The officer course trains soldiers in the skills and knowledge required to be commanders. The weapons course drills soldiers in all types of foreign weapons, from rifles to antitank guns; students of the engineering course are taught field construction and fortification, land mine warfare, target analysis, and demolitions.

Secret communications are also vital for the resupply, reinforcement, and escape of Special Forces teams behind enemy lines. To pass the signals course, the students must show that they can build radio antennae, make and break secret codes, and use specialized communications equipment. At the end of the course, the students must be able to send and receive Morse code at a minimum speed of eight words per minute.

The culmination exercise is the last phase of selection and is designed to test the skills learned on the other two phases. The Robin Sage Field Training Exercise lasts 19 days and simulates a realistic wartime operation. Organized into "A-Teams", the students must train a mock guerrilla force comprised of civilians from local families. Once trained and organized, the "guerrillas" are led on a series of raids and ambushes against the **82nd Airborne Division**, who play the forces of the "evil dictator."

Here, two U.S. soldiers practice unarmed combat at the Hunter Army Base near Savannah, Georgia. Special Forces troops draw on a variety of techniques, including karate and kung fu.

Survivors of the "Q" Course are awarded their green berets. The "Special Forces" shoulder tabs are awarded only to those candidates who pass the final two phases: Language Training and Survival, Evasion, Resistance, and Escape (SERE).

Soldiers training for induction to the Special Forces carry heavy weights, designed to simulate carrying an injured comrade from the battlefield, using a frame of poles suspended on their shoulders.

A change of command ceremony at Fort Bragg, North Carolina. Elite soldiers are very proud of who they are and the tradition of their unit.

MORSE CODE

Morse code is taught to all Special Forces soldiers. Invented in 1867 by Samuel Morse, the code is made up of a series of lines and dots, each of which stand for a letter of the alphabet. Messages can be relayed audibly (by a Morse code signaling machine) or visually, by flashing a light or waving flags.

U.S. NAVY SEALs SELECTION

The Navy SEALs are undoubtedly the most highly trained of the modern U.S. elite forces. SEALs stands for Sea, Air, and Land, and the selection courses produce people who can survive in the most hostile environments of all these terrains. But many do not make it through the training.

Applicants for the SEALs must be qualified in a specialty field such as medical care, computers and communications, and engineering or electronics. They also have to pass a rigorous diving medical, and have produced high scores on physical and mental aptitude tests. Entry into this elite of elites is by means of the infamous Basic Underwater Demolition/SEAL (**BUDS**) training program.

The first four weeks of BUDS are tough by any standard. Every element of the training is competitive as the different teams race against the clock and each other. After a two-week warm-up period, the class learns how to handle different small boats before turning to beach reconnaissance and long-range land patrol skills. Perfection is achieved by the endless repetition of exercises using live ammunition with the constant pressure to improve accuracy, timing, and teamwork. While most of the public think of the SEALs as combat **frogmen**, the U.S. Navy does not share this misconception. As their name implies, these operators are trained

A SEAL frogman emerging from the water at Coronado, North Island, California. The weapons used by the SEALs must be totally waterproof.

to fight in any environment, including far behind enemy lines on land, as recent operations in the 1991 **Gulf War** demonstrated. This basic phase of selection and training culminates in an ultra-tough training period. More than half of the people on the course have now left in one of two ways, either by being terminated by the course instructors or by ringing a brass bell three times to announce their voluntary withdrawal from BUDS.

Specialized training begins on Week Six with long swims and free-diving exercises to boost confidence. To remain on BUDS, every candidate must complete a 150-foot (45-m) underwater swim and a five-mile (8-km) marathon on the surface. The course

Preparing to jump from a MH-53 helicopter during exercises in the Pacific. Once the SEAL hits the water, the hard work really begins.

During "drownproofing," a SEAL must swim, float, and dive with his ankles and wrists bound.

then splits into pairs for diving training. The instruction starts with sports scuba equipment but soon progresses to the LARV-5 Draeger re-breathing rig, which eliminates telltale bubbles that enemy sentries might spot from the shore. Swimming in pitch-black murky water, with only a compass to guide them, the students must show that they can cope with possible diving emergencies.

The students are also introduced to the array of vehicles that may carry them close to their target. Six nuclear submarines have been converted for SEAL operations. Each of these vessels can carry pods containing diving vehicles capable of taking the teams through treacherous tides and currents to the enemy coast. On the surface, the craft navigate by computerized satellite systems. Once the target is reached, the craft sinks below the harbor defenses. Underwater, the students use sophisticated microphones to talk to each other and their parent submarine. The device is powered by batteries and has an effective

SEAL divers undertake repairs on a stricken submarine in the Pacific. They often train in pitch-black water conditions for these exercises.

underwater range of 30,000 feet (9,150 m). The sabotage of enemy shipping is now accomplished with a range of light plastic limpet mines (explosives that can be stuck to the side of boats) and demolition charges. But if the target cannot be reached successfully, the diving vehicles can fire sophisticated long-range Mark 37 torpedoes.

After undergoing rigorous specialized underwater warfare training, the students complete a parachute course in which they learn how to make "wet" drops into the sea with their equipment. SEAL operations may take the teams inland and far from the sea. Consequently, after qualifying, many SEAL team members progress to High-Altitude, Low-Opening (**HALO**) and High-Altitude, High-Opening (**HAHO**) parachuting. HALO, or military freefall, lets the parachutist descend undetected through the enemy's radar. The parachutist falls from high altitude and

Land raids usually take place at dawn or dusk. The poor light, coupled with their camouflage clothing, decreases the likelihood of detection by enemy forces. This technique was used to great effect in Vietnam.

opens his parachute only at the last minute. However, leaving an aircraft from an altitude in excess of 33,000 feet (10,000 m) has its drawbacks. At this height, frostbite will occur in minutes and there is so little oxygen that the parachutist must wear a protective suit and carry an air/oxygen tank. To this must be added the main and reserve parachutes, an altimeter, weapon, and a backpack or bergen. Wearing this cumbersome mass of specialist equipment creates great problems with stability. If the parachutist was to start spinning in midair, the consequences could be disastrous—at best, he could hope to pull the ripcord and float down in clear view of the enemy.

Another high-altitude parachuting technique, which avoids the necessity of aircraft entering enemy air space, is HAHO. This technique was reputedly used to insert teams into Kuwait and southern Iraq during Operation **"Desert Storm"** in the Gulf War. HAHO parachutists leave the aircraft at high altitudes. They deploy the parachute immediately and then glide down onto a chosen drop

zone (DZ) 30 to 35 miles (50–60 km) from where they jumped out of the aircraft. This is a reasonably simple technique that avoids many of the problems of HALO. However, in practice there have been difficulties in actually finding the DZ, particularly during night jumps. This problem has recently been solved with a small satellite navigation pack that guides the parachutist to his DZ.

All training courses after selection for the U.S. Navy SEALs are held at the Special Warfare Center and School at Fort Bragg, North Carolina, where the operators are taught most of the subjects found on Special Forces selection. SEAL training is never complete but is deemed satisfactory after the candidates have completed overseas jungle, desert, and arctic warfare training. Such is the "finishing school" for those who are asked to handle some of the most dangerous operations in the world.

As we have seen, it takes a rare type of person to complete the training for elite units. However, elite soldiers are not superhumans. In fact, they are people who have dedicated themselves to excellence. They stand as examples of what human beings can achieve if they really push themselves to do their best.

STAYING AFLOAT WITH THE SEALs

The SEALs have a special technique for staying alive in the water for long periods of time. Lie face down in the water with your arms and legs fully extended like a star. Push down your arms to raise the head and take a breath of air. Hold your breath and relax again. You will float just below the surface even when wearing heavy clothing and boots. Blow the air out gently until you need a breath again and once again push down with the arms and raise the head.

GLOSSARY

Aerobic Exercises that make you breathe harder and take in more oxygen, and also increase the speed of your heart.

Anatomy The study of the structure of the human body.

Anaerobic Physical exercises that do not result in an increased intake of oxygen.

BUDS An acronym that stands for Basic Underwater Demolitions/SEAL. It is part of the SEALs training course.

Continuation Training The part of SAS training that teaches the recruits the basic skills of an elite soldier.

Desert Storm The operation during the Gulf War in which the U.S. and allied troops pushed Iraqi forces out of Kuwait.

Frogmen Soldiers equipped with face mask, fins, and breathing apparatus for the purposes of underwater military reconaissance.

Gulf War The war in 1990–91 that took place after Iraq invaded Kuwait. The U.S. led an international force to repel the Iraqis.

HAHO An acronym for High-Altitude High-Opening parachuting.

HALO An acronym for High-Altitude Low-Opening parachuting.

Kit Equipment carried by soldiers during training and on missions.

Ligaments The parts of the human body that connect the muscles to the bones.

Log race A part of training for the Parachute Regiment in which the recruits carry a heavy log for one and three-quarters miles (2.8 km).

"P" Company The section of British Parachute Regiment training that focuses on testing the applicants' endurance.

Physiology The science of how the bodies of living creatures work.

Red Beret The nickname of the soldiers of the Parachute Regiment, named after the color of their berets.

RV Rendezvous or meeting point.

SAS Special Air Service, the British Army's most elite force.

SEALs An elite unit in the U.S. Navy. Their name stands for Sea, Air, and Land.

Special Forces An elite division of the U.S. Army. They are distinguished by a green beret which is awarded to soldiers upon successful completion of their training course, Special Forces Assessment and Selection (SFAS).

Spetsnaz An elite Russian army unit.

Stamina Staying power, endurance.

Steeplechase The name of a special assault course used by the Parachute Regiment (Paras).

Suppleness The ability to bend and move easily.

Tendons A tough cord of white tissue that connects muscles in the body to bone.

Trainasium A high obstacle course used by the British Paras to test whether they can conquer a fear of heights.

82nd Airborne Division An elite parachute-trained division of the U.S. Army.

0700 hours To avoid confusion, the army measures time according to the 24-hour clock, so 0700 hours is 7 A.M. and 2000 hours is 8 A.M.

RECRUITMENT INFORMATION

U.S. Special Forces

The Special Forces take only people who are already soldiers. They:

- Must be U.S. male citizens.
- Must have minimum GT score of 110; waiverable to 100.
- Must be High School graduate or GED equivalent.
- airborne qualified or volunteer for airborne training.
- Must be able to swim 170 feet (45 meters) wearing boots and battle dress uniform (BDU) at the start of the Special Forces Qualification Course.
- Must score a minimum of 229 points on the Army physical fitness test (APFT). This is made up of three exercises: push-ups, sit-ups, and a two-mile run. Each discipline affords a maximum score of 100. (The number of repetitions and time for the run vary according to the height and weight of the applicant).
- Pass the Special Forces physical.
- In terms of rank, they must be Special (E-4) through Sergeant First Class (E-7) or a promotable First Lieutenant or Captain.

Enlisted individuals must also have a high school diploma or the equivalent. Selection for Special Forces training is based on a 25-day Special Forces Assessment and Selection (SFAS) course. If you pass, you go onto proper Special Forces training, which could last up to one year, plus four to six months for language training and three weeks for the Survival, Evade, Resist, and Escape (SERE) Course.

If you want to find out more about the U.S. Special Forces, go to your nearest U.S. Army recruiting office or visit the following web sites:

http://www.goarmy.com
http://www.specialforces.net
http://www,users.aol.com/armysof1/SpecialForces.html
http://www.members.nbci.com/raymondluk

Special Air Service (SAS)

To enter the Special Air Service, you have to be a serving soldier in the British Army of commonwealth forces. (Sometimes other foreign nationals are considered; always check first.) You have to have a good record of soldiering and also have about three years of military service remaining.

Selection for the SAS is very tough. Courses are run twice a year, in the summer and winter. Few people succeed. Of every 150 people who start the selection course, only about 15 people actually pass, sometimes fewer. For those who are considering entering the SAS, a career in the British Army is the first step. To find out about the British Army, go to any Armed Forces Recruiting Office in the U.K. (They can be found in most towns and cities.) The recruiting officers there will tell you all about the army careers that are available and help you to choose from literally hundreds of jobs and roles. For more information, go to the following websites:

http://www.army.mod.uk

http://www.specwarnet.com/europe/sas.htm

http://www.geocities.com/alli_cool_dood/

U.S. Navy SEALs

To enter SEAL training, you must pass a rigorous physical test, especially of your swimming, and also do well in the Armed Services Vocational Aptitude Battery (ASVAB) intelligence test. You must be a U.S. citizen and up to 28 years old. The initial fitness test involves a series of exercises punctuated by short rests:

- 500-yard (500-meter) swim using breast and/or sidestroke in $12^{1}/_{2}$ minutes.
  10-minute rest.
- Perform a minimum of 42 push-ups in two minutes.
  Two-minute rest.

- Perform a minimum of 50 sit-ups in two minutes.
  Two-minute rest.
- Perform a minimum of six chin-ups (there is no time limit).
  10-minute rest.
- Run a mile and a half (2.4 km) wearing boots and long pants
  in $11^{1}/_{2}$ minutes.

If you pass this, you then go on to Basic Underwater Demolitions/SEAL training (BUDS). This is one of the toughest training courses in the world, and up to 80 percent of people fail. It can last up to one year and trains you in every form of combat, but especially underwater/marine missions. There are three main phases to BUDS: basic conditioning (nine weeks), diving (seven weeks), and demolitions and land warfare (nine weeks). If you do go for the SEALs, make sure that you are very fit before you start!

There are 2,300 qualified SEALs currently in service.

To find out more about the SEALs entry requirements and training go to:
http://www.sealchallenge.navy.mil
http://www.navyseals.com
http://www.chinfo.navy.mil
http://www.defenselink.mil

FURTHER READING

Brehm, Jack. *That Others May Live: The True Story of a PJ, a Member of America's Most Daring Rescue Force*. Victoria, B.C., Canada: Crown Publications, 2000.

Chalker, Dennis C. *The United States Navy SEALs Workout Guide: The Exercises and Fitness Programs Used by the U.S. Navy SEALS and BUDS Training*. London: William Morrow & Co., 1998.

Da Cruz, Daniel. *Boot*. New York: St. Martin's Paperbacks, 1987.

Davies, Barry. *Joining the SAS—How to get in and what it's like*. London: Pan Books, 1998.

Foster, Nigel. *The Making of a Royal Marines Commando*. London: Pan Books, 1987.

McNab, Chris. *Endurance Techniques*. London: Brown Books, 2001.

Stillwell, Alexander. *The Encyclopedia of Survival Techniques*. New York: Lyons Press, 2000.

Thompson, Peter. *The Real Insider's Guide to Military Basic Training: A Recruit's Guide of Advice and Hints to Make It Through Boot Camp*. Parkland, Fla.: Upublish.com, 1998.

Weale, Adrian. *Fighting Fit—The Complete SAS Fitness Training Guide*. London: Orion, 2001.

Wiseman, John. *The SAS Personal Trainer*. London: Lewis International Inc., 1998.

ABOUT THE AUTHOR

Dr. Chris McNab has written and edited numerous books on military history and elite forces survival. His publications to date include *German Paratroopers of World War II, The Illustrated History of the Vietnam War, First Aid Survival Manual*, and *Special Forces Endurance Techniques*, as well as many articles and features in other works. Forthcoming publications include books on the SAS, while Chris's wider research interests lie in literature and ancient history. Chris lives in South Wales, U.K.

INDEX

References in italics refer to illustrations

abseiling *39*
aerobic exercise 15–16
aggression 27
anaerobic exercise 15
arms *see* weapons
assault courses 32–33

Basic Underwater
Demolition/SEAL
training program
(BUDS) 51–57
battles *see* fighting
boat handling (U.S.
Navy SEALs) 51
British Army Regimental
Signalers 37

calisthenics *14*, 15
capture evasion 38–40
choosing elite soldiers
19–25
circuit training 16
clothing 28–29
  U.S. Special Forces *43*
combat medicine (U.S.
Special Forces) 45–46
combat survival 38
commitment *22*
communications (U.S.
Special Forces) 45, 46
confidence 23, 25, 40
conflict *see* fighting
constructive criticism 21
Continuation Training
(SAS) 37–40
Culmination Exercises
(U.S. Special Forces) 45,
46–48
cycling 12, 15

demolitions training
(SAS) 38
dependability 27
diving 53
diving vehicles 53–54

endurance 30, 33, 41
engineering (U.S. Special
Forces) 45, 46

"Fan Dance" 36
fear, overcoming
24–25, 40
fighting
  Gulf War 41, 52, 56

Vietnam War
42, 43, *55*
"fire-running" 26
first aid
  SAS 37–38
  U.S. Special Forces
  45–46
fitness *see* physical fitness

glossary 58–59
Green Berets 48
Gulf War 41, 52, 56
guns *see* weapons
gyms 11–12

handling panic 25
helicopters
  MH-53 helicopter *52*
helpful criticism 21

initiative 27
intelligence 27, *32*, 43
Internet addresses 62
interrogation, resistance
to 38–40

jungle training 40

kit 28–29
  U.S. Special Forces *43*

lifting weights 16–17
"log race" *29*, 30
"Long Drag" 36

M16 rifle *34*
Mark 37 torpedoes 54
martial arts 15
medical skill (SAS)
37–38
mental preparation
19–25
MH-53 helicopter *52*
Military Occupational
Skill (U.S. Special
Forces) 45
"milling" *31*
Morse code 37, *38*, 49
motivation 12, 19–20,
27, 35, 45
"mudwalking" *12*

navigation (SAS) 35

officer course (U.S.

Special Forces) 46

pacing yourself 11–15
panic 25
Parachute Regiment
(British) 28–33
parachuting courses 40
  U.S. Navy SEALs
  54–57
  U.S. Special Forces *44*
patrol tactics (SAS) 37
physical fitness *6*, 8–17,
19–20, 27, 28–33
  SAS 35–37
  U.S. Special Forces
  43–45
positive thinking
19, *21*, 23
preparing the mind
19–25
push-ups *14*, *18*

Ranger School 43
recruitment information
60–62
resistance to interro-
gation 38–40
rowing 15
running 15, *20*

Sabre Squadrons 40–41
SAS (British)
  humor 23
  recruitment
  information 61
  selection 34–41
selection procedures
27–33
  SAS (British) 34–41
  U.S. Navy SEALs
  50–57
  U.S. Special Forces
  42–49
self-confidence
23, 25, 40
self-discipline 27
self-hypnosis *21*
self-motivation 12,
19–20, 35, 45
sense of humor 23
signaling 37
  U.S. Special Forces 46
Small Unit Tactics (U.S.
Special Forces) 45
Special Forces

Assessment and Selection
(SFAS) 45
Special Forces
Qualification Course ("Q
Course") 45–48
Special Warfare Center
and School 57
stamina 10–11
"Steeplechase" 30
strength 10–11
stress 9–10
stretching 14, 17
submarines 53
suppleness 10–11
swimming 12, 15, 43,
52–53

team spirit 27, 51
Test Week (SAS) 35–36
"Trainasium" 31–32
training 28–33
  "fire-running" *26*
  mental preparation
  19–25
  physical 8–17
  SAS 34–41
  U.S. Navy SEALs
  50–57
  U.S. Special Forces
  42–49

underwater warfare
training 53–54
uniform 28–29
  U.S. Special Forces 43
U.S. Navy SEALs 50–57
  recruitment
  information 61–62
U.S. Special Forces
42–49
  recruitment
  information 60

Vietnam War *42*, 43, *55*

walking 11, 12
war *see* fighting
warming up 12–14
weapons
  M16 rifle *34*
  Mark 37 torpedoes 54
  training in (U.S.
  Special Forces) 45, 46
web sites 62
weight training 16–17